MW01595063

depth Small Group
le Studies

TUDY
UIDE

rt One of a
vo-Part Study

LUKE (Part One)

taking up the Master's mission

Joel Kok

Luke

Christian Resources

Grand Rapids, Michigan

Cover photo: EyeWire

Faith Alive Christian Resources published by CRC Publications.
Word Alive: In-depth Small Group Bible Studies
Luke: Taking Up the Master's Mission (Study Guide), Part One of a Two-Part Study, © 1997, 2002 by CRC Publications, 2850 Kalamazoo Ave. SE, Grand Rapids, MI 49560. All rights reserved. With the exception of brief excerpts for review purposes, no part of this book may be reproduced in any manner whatsoever without written permission from the publisher. Printed in the United States of America on recycled paper.

Note: This study material is revised from the Revelation Series format in which it was published in 1997.

We welcome your comments. Call us at 1-800-333-8300 or e-mail us at editors@faithaliveresources.org.

ISBN 1-56212-852-3

10 9 8 7 6 5 4 3 2 1

Contents

Introduction 5

Lesson 1: A Certain Knowledge of Christ 7
Lesson 2: A Kingdom of War and Peace 15
Lesson 3: Jesus and the Holy Spirit 23
Lesson 4: The Son in the Wilderness 31
Lesson 5: Listening to the Enemy 39
Lesson 6: A Kingdom of Blessing and Woe 47
Lesson 7: The Reward of Discipleship 55

Evaluation 63

Introduction

Sometimes we pick up a book or go to a movie again and again because we know we'll get more out of it each time we read or view it. We do this even though we know the end of the story. We want to remind ourselves of the important things we've learned, and we have a sense that there's more to be learned—perhaps at a deeper level or in a detail we might have missed or forgotten.

We do this with the Bible too, and rightly so—not because we view God's revelation as "just a story." We do it because we know there's so much in it that God wants us to know about real life, the life God gives, and because we know God works through it to help us stay in tune with God. We do it not just because the Bible reveals the fascinating drama of our salvation but, even more, because the Holy Spirit leads us into it and uses it to train us in what we know, deep down, is the way for us to live (see Rom. 1:20; 1 Tim. 3:16-17).

As we begin this Bible study on the gospel of Luke, we're looking again into a story we've heard before—perhaps hundreds of times. We know the end of the story. Many of us know lots of the details that make it a fascinating story. Many of us even know some of the themes that tie in to make it the crux of God's story of salvation to a hopeless humanity.

It's far more than "just a story," however. The life story of Jesus Christ is God's revelation to us about who Jesus is and what he did. It's God's revelation to us about why Jesus came and what that means for us.

In this study we'll talk about all this from the perspective God has given us through Luke. And we're going to begin near the end of the story, after Jesus' resurrection, so that we can look back on Jesus' life through the lens of "what [is] said in all the Scriptures" about him (Luke 24:27)—namely, that "the Christ [had] to suffer . . . and then enter his glory" (24:26). Further, as we examine the life and purpose of Jesus as the Son of God, Prince of Peace, Master, Savior, and exalted Lord, we'll also be focusing on how God wants us, as Jesus' disciples, to take up our Master's mission.

—Paul Faber, for Faith Alive Christian Resources

Joel Kok, author of this study guide and the accompanying leader's guide, is a Christian Reformed pastor in Broomall, Pennsylvania. He has also served as a pastor in Ames, Iowa, and as an adjunct professor of Bible at Eastern University, St. David, Pennsylvania, and at Eastern Baptist Theological Seminary, Wynnewood, Pennsylvania.

How can Jesus'
ministry guide
us in our
mission?

1

A Certain Knowledge of Christ

In a Nutshell

The purpose of our study of Luke is to emphasize "the importance of the earthly ministry of Jesus for the continuing life of the Church." James S. Stewart argues for this approach to the gospels in his book *The Life and Teaching of Jesus Christ.* What Stewart did for an earlier generation needs to be repeated for this generation and, indeed, for every generation of Christians. Whatever our situation—however different it may be from that of first-century Palestine—the words and deeds of Jesus can still guide the church in its mission. For, as Stewart also observes, "in the pages of the Gospels men and women still encounter the living Christ."

Luke 1:1-4

¹Many have undertaken to draw up an account of the things that have been fulfilled among us, ²just as they were handed down to us by those who from the first were eyewitnesses and servants of the word. ³Therefore, since I myself have carefully investigated everything from the beginning, it seemed good also to me to write an orderly account for you, most excellent Theophilus, ⁴so that you may know the certainty of the things you have been taught.

24:13-35

¹³Now that same day two of them were going to a village called Emmaus, about seven miles from Jerusalem. ¹⁴They were talking with each other about everything that had happened. ¹⁵As they talked and discussed these things with each other, Jesus himself came up and walked along with them; ¹⁶but they were kept from recognizing him.

¹⁷He asked them, "What are you discussing together as you walk along?"

They stood still, their faces downcast. ¹⁸One of them, named Cleopas, asked him, "Are you only a visitor to Jerusalem and do not know the things that have happened there in these days?"

¹⁹"What things?" he asked.

"About Jesus of Nazareth," they replied. "He was a prophet, powerful in word and deed before God and all the people. 20The chief priests and our rulers handed him over to be sentenced to death, and they crucified him; 21but we had hoped that he was the one who was going to redeem Israel. And what is more, it is the third day since all this took place. 22In addition, some of our women amazed us. They went to the tomb early this morning 23but didn't find his body. They came and told us that they had seen a vision of angels, who said he was alive. 24Then some of our companions went to the tomb and found it just as the women had said, but him they did not see."

25He said to them, "How foolish you are, and how slow of heart to believe all that the prophets have spoken! 26Did not the Christ have to suffer these things and then enter his glory?" 27And beginning with Moses and all the Prophets, he explained to them what was said in all the Scriptures concerning himself.

28As they approached the village to which they were going, Jesus acted as if he were going farther. 29But they urged him strongly, "Stay with us, for it is nearly evening; the day is almost over." So he went in to stay with them.

30When he was at the table with them, he took bread, gave thanks, broke it and began to give it to them. 31Then their eyes were opened and they recognized him, and he disappeared from their sight. 32They asked each other, "Were not our hearts burning within us while he talked with us on the road and opened the Scriptures to us?"

33They got up and returned at once to Jerusalem. There they found the Eleven and those with them, assembled together 34and saying, "It is true! The Lord has risen and has appeared to Simon." 35Then the two told what had happened on the way, and how Jesus was recognized by them when he broke the bread.

Additional reading: Luke 9:51-62; 18:31-34
See also Acts 1:1-8

Solid Instruction

Luke wrote his gospel so that someone named Theophilus could "know the certainty" of the things he had been taught (Luke 1:4). We do not know who Theophilus was. We do not even know whether he was a Christian. From the way Luke addresses this person, however, we can guess that Theophilus had received some instruction in the Christian faith but needed to deepen and solidify his knowledge.

In this respect, Theophilus represents all kinds of people who read the gospel of Luke today. Theophilus represents spiritual seekers, who have heard of Jesus but don't know the biblical teachings about him. Theophilus represents young Christians, who have converted to Christ but don't understand very well what it means to follow him. Theophilus also represents longtime believers, who continually need to deepen their roots in Jesus and in his Word.

We all need the solid instruction about Jesus that Luke offers in his gospel. Only through disciplined learning about Christ can we become the good soil that produces the crop our Lord is looking for as he sows the seed of the Word throughout the world (see 8:4-15). In this lesson we'll take a look at the structure of the gospel of Luke and explore how this structure leads us from distorted expectations about Jesus to a true recognition of Jesus and the salvation he brings.

The Christ-Pattern in Luke and the Bible

The gospel of Luke can be divided into three main sections. The first section stretches from Jesus' infancy through his ministry in Galilee (1:5-9:50). The second section describes Jesus' determined traveling to Jerusalem (9:51-19:27). The third section describes Jesus' entrance into Jerusalem, where he is crucified and then rises from the dead and ascends to heaven (19:28-24:53). The pivot on which this story turns is Luke 9:51: "As the time approached for him to be taken up to heaven, Jesus resolutely set out for Jerusalem." Jesus had to steel himself to journey to the city he loved because he knew the cross awaited him there (see 13:34-35; 19:41-42).

As we will note in lesson 2, the cross overshadows Jesus' life even from the time of his birth. The way of the cross—a way of suffering love that leads to glory—shapes Jesus' mission from beginning to end. Right after Peter confesses that Jesus is the Christ, for example, Jesus explains what being the Christ means: "The Son of Man must suffer many things and be rejected by the elders, chief priests and teachers of the law, and he must be killed and on the third day be raised to life" (9:22). This Christ-pattern—humility and death leading to resurrection and exaltation—arises for Jesus from the teachings of Scripture. Twice on the first Easter, Jesus explained to his disciples that, according to the Scriptures, the Christ first had to suffer and then had to enter his glory (24:25-27, 45-46). Luke structures his gospel to make this Christ-pattern clear to his readers.

The Kingdom and the Cross

Luke needed to make this Christ-pattern as clear as possible because even Jesus' disciples found it hard to understand. According to Luke, when Jesus announced that he would suffer and die in Jerusalem, "the disciples did not understand any of this. Its meaning was hidden from them, and they did not know what he was talking about" (18:34; see 9:45). Even after Jesus' crucifixion and resurrection, the disciples did not understand. With holy impatience, therefore, Jesus said to the Emmaus-goers, "How foolish you are, and how slow of heart to believe all that the prophets have spoken!" (24:25). Then Jesus "opened the Scriptures" (24:32) to show them the Christ-pattern in the Bible. Later Jesus "opened [the disciples'] minds so they could understand the Scriptures" (24:45) according to this same pattern of suffering and death that leads to glory and exaltation.

Luke emphasizes the cross because, apart from a theology of the cross, Jesus' disciples misunderstood the salvation Jesus had brought. Notice how Cleopas and his companion, not recognizing the risen Lord, attempted to explain to Jesus himself who Jesus was. They said, "We had hoped that he was the one who was going to redeem Israel" (24:21). In other words, these followers of Christ had hoped Jesus would be a king who would restore Israel to the glory days of David and Solomon. With expectations of militaristic and nationalistic glory dominating their view of God's kingdom, these travelers to Emmaus could not understand how Jesus could be a king—a Christ—who would suffer and die before rising from the dead. They needed to have their eyes opened to the Christ-pattern before they could truly recognize Jesus (see 24:31).

The same is true for Jesus' followers today. We all share with Cleopas and his companion a tendency to project onto Jesus our distorted expectations and false hopes for worldly glory. The Christ-pattern shatters those illusions. But in place of our dashed hopes Jesus offers us something better. He shows his love for us by dying for us, and then he meets us on the other side of the grave to lead us into everlasting fellowship with him. This loving fellowship is stronger than death and extends to all peoples. And the true kingdom that Jesus brings, God's kingdom of the cross, can inspire us to give up anything to gain life with Jesus (see 9:24).

By recognizing the Christ-pattern, we can follow Jesus' way of the cross while knowing that God is at work in us "to do immeasurably more than all we ask or imagine" (Eph. 3:20). Let's study the gospel of Luke with this in mind. And let's ask the Lord to open the Scriptures to us in a way that sets "our hearts burning within us" (Luke 24:32).

Additional Notes

1:1—"Many" seems almost certainly to have included the gospel of Mark. Scholars also often refer to another source, which they call "Q" (from the German word for "source"); this source was apparently used by both Matthew and Luke. We can only speculate about such a source, however, since no manuscript has been found to verify its existence.

1:2—The "eyewitnesses and servants of the word" are people Luke interviewed, perhaps when he was in Jerusalem as a companion of Paul (see Acts 21-23). Kenneth E. Bailey makes the point that these people "may have been given the specific task of preserving the Jesus tradition."

24:18—"Cleopas" is similar to the name "Clopas," cited in John 19:25. The apostle John refers to Clopas's wife, Mary, standing near the cross. This raises the possibility that the Emmaus-goers might have been Clopas and Mary.

24:26—Jesus asks, "Did not the Christ have to suffer?" The Greek verb *dei*, translated here as "have," conveys a situation of necessity. The same word is used in Luke 9:22; 17:25; 22:37; 24:7—each time related to the necessity of the Christ's suffering. This is not a necessity of fate but a necessity of love. When you love someone the way Jesus loved sinners, you must suffer with them.

24:35—"When he broke the bread" seems intended to help the reader recall other situations in which Jesus broke bread (see 9:10-17; 22:19) and, in this way, it takes on liturgical significance. Luke's word choice, however, is best translated as "in the breaking of the bread" (NRSV).

GENERAL DISCUSSION

1. What are the greatest challenges facing the Christian church today? Where do we look for guidance in facing these challenges?

2. Cite two or three passages Jesus might have pointed to when he "explained . . . what was said in all the Scriptures concerning himself" (Luke 24:27).

3. In what ways can knowing about the Christ-pattern help us in our study of Luke's gospel?

4. Luke refers to "many" others who have written accounts about Jesus (Luke 1:1). Who are those others? Why do we have more than one gospel account?

5. Compare Luke 1:1-4 with Acts 1:1-3. What continuity do you see between the openings of Luke and Acts? What discontinuity do you see?

6. Note Luke 24:16 and 24:31. What kept Cleopas and the other disciple from recognizing Jesus? What opened their eyes?

7. Reflect further on the travelers' hope that Jesus would be the one to redeem Israel. What versions of that sort of hope do we have today?

SMALL GROUP SESSION IDEAS

Opening (5-10 minutes)
Pray/Worship—Open your first session of this study with a prayer for God's guidance as you look to the Scriptures to learn about "taking up the Master's mission." Thank God for bringing your group together for this study, and ask that this course may help each person in your group to strive to grow more and more like Christ.

Begin a time of worship, if you wish, by reflecting quietly on ways in which you need to become more like Christ. Take a minute or two for a time of silent prayer. Then sing together one or two prayerful hymns or praise songs that call us to dedicate ourselves to Christ and his kingdom—for example, "Lord, I Want to Be a Christian" and "Seek Ye First the Kingdom." Pray again together, asking God's Spirit to help you understand how you might pattern yourselves after Christ in your daily living.

Share—If your group is used to meeting together, you'll want to take some time to catch up on how things have been going since you last met. If some or all of you haven't been part of this group before, you'll want to introduce yourselves and perhaps each share something about yourself that you'd like the others in the group to know. For starters, you may want to share with each other the expectations you have as you begin this study of *Luke: Taking Up the Master's Mission.*

Focus—The focus question in each lesson is designed to help you begin thinking about the lesson material and how it affects you. Ask yourself the following focus question as you begin this session: *What does the Christ-pattern have to do with me?*

Growing (35-50 minutes)
Read (optional)—You may want to read Luke 1:1-4 and 24:13-35 together (as well as the other passages and study guide notes) before moving into a discussion time.

Discuss—Before choosing from the following process questions for your discussion, you'll want to work through some of the General Discussion questions—especially questions 1, 2, 3, and 6, which relate closely to the questions that follow.

- Share with the others in your group how it helps you to know what the Old Testament says about Christ before he came.

- Think of an experience in which you've had your eyes opened to see Jesus in your life. Share that experience with your group, if you're comfortable doing so.

- When you think about what Christ has done for you, what effect does that have on you?

- What sorts of self-sacrifice do you need to make in order to reflect the Christ-pattern in your personal life? As part of your small group? In facing challenges in the church today?

Goalsetting (5 minutes)
Try to work on the following goal in the coming week:

- Here's what I need to do to live by the Christ-pattern:

Closing (5-10 minutes)

Preparing for Prayer—This is a time for sharing praise items and concerns that you'd like the others in your group to bring before God in prayer for you, both now and during the coming week. You may also want to ask for prayers for God's help in meeting the goal you've set during this session.

Prayer—Close your meeting with prayer, asking the Lord to help you live by the model Christ showed in his life of suffering and glory among us. Everyone may join in with prayer concerns and praises. Then ask for God's blessing and guidance in the coming weeks as you study more about the gospel of Luke together.

Before you part till your next meeting, you may want to join together in a reading of the Apostles' Creed, paying special attention to the section about Christ and all he has done for us. Wish each other God's blessing till you meet for your next lesson.

*We have to fight
in a Christlike
way to have the
peace of God.*

2

LUKE 2:1-20

A Kingdom of War and Peace

In a Nutshell

The story of salvation is the story of God's overcoming rebellion to remake this earth and its universe into the kingdom of peace it's intended to be. And the birth of Jesus is the turning point in this redemptive warfare. Jesus, the true King, is born to rescue the universe from the diabolical rule of Satan, the false king. But there's a surprising twist: God overcomes this world in an "upside-down" way.

Luke 2:1-20

¹In those days Caesar Augustus issued a decree that a census should be taken of the entire Roman world. ²(This was the first census that took place while Quirinius was governor of Syria.) ³And everyone went to his own town to register.

⁴So Joseph also went up from the town of Nazareth in Galilee to Judea, to Bethlehem the town of David, because he belonged to the house and line of David. ⁵He went there to register with Mary, who was pledged to be married to him and was expecting a child. ⁶While they were there, the time came for the baby to be born, ⁷and she gave birth to her firstborn, a son. She wrapped him in cloths and placed him in a manger, because there was no room for them in the inn.

⁸And there were shepherds living out in the fields nearby, keeping watch over their flocks at night. ⁹An angel of the Lord appeared to them, and the glory of the Lord shone around them, and they were terrified. ¹⁰But the angel said to them, "Do not be afraid. I bring you good news of great joy that will be for all the people. ¹¹Today in the town of David a Savior has been born to you; he is Christ the Lord. ¹²This will be a sign to you: You will find a baby wrapped in cloths and lying in a manger."

¹³Suddenly a great company of the heavenly host appeared with the angel, praising God and saying,

¹⁴ "Glory to God in the highest,
and on earth peace to men on
whom his favor rests."

¹⁵When the angels had left them and gone into heaven, the shepherds said to one another, "Let's go to Bethlehem and see this thing that has happened, which the Lord has told us about."

16So they hurried off and found Mary and Joseph, and the baby, who was lying in the manger. 17When they had seen him, they spread the word concerning what had been told them about this child, 18and all who heard it were amazed at what the shepherds said to them. 19But Mary treasured up all these things and pondered them in her heart. 20The shepherds returned, glorifying and praising God for all the things they had heard and seen, which were just as they had been told.

Additional reading: Luke 9:1-6; 10:1-7, 17-20
See also Isaiah 9:1-7; Revelation 12

Mixed Feelings at Christmas

Every year at Christmastime, it seems, the air is filled with songs about peace and news about war. This contrast can trouble believers in Christ and his kingdom. We want to echo the angelic song from Luke 2:14 about peace on earth, but how can we do that with so many reports of violence and injustice at home and around the world? Often this question becomes personal. The angel who appeared to the shepherds on the first Christmas announced "good news of great joy that will be for all the people" (Luke 2:10). Yet we know all too well that people we love and even we ourselves can be heavily burdened by grief and distress. A preacher-writer named Hugh O'Driscoll observes that the contrast between the glad message of Jesus' birth and the sad conditions of many people in this world can lead some to fall into depression and even think about suicide at Christmastime. What can we make of this mixed-up reality?

Universal War and the Prince of Peace

One way to wrestle with issues like this is to recognize that the Bible describes our world as a universe at war. Creatures, both human beings and fallen angels, have rebelled against their Creator, and this conflict ravages the earth. The biblical story of salvation is the story of God's overcoming this rebellion in order to remake the earth into the kingdom of peace God intends all creation to be. And the birth of Jesus is the turning point in this redemptive warfare. Jesus, the true King, is born to rescue the universe from the diabolical rule of Satan, the false king (1 John 3:8). Christmas celebrates the truth that, as C. S. Lewis puts it, "God has landed on this enemy-occupied world in human form." King Jesus will indeed establish peace on earth, but his followers will have to fight in a Christlike way to enter the peace of God.

This biblical worldview helps us understand the military images we find throughout Scripture. Revelation 12, for example, looks back on the temptation story in Genesis 3 and on the Christmas story. The ancient serpent who tempted Adam and Eve did so as part of a "war in heaven" (Rev. 12:7), in which Michael and God's other obedient angels hurled Satan and his allies out of heaven and "to the earth" (12:9). Refusing to surrender, Satan, depicted as a dragon, continued the spiritual warfare by leading "the whole world astray" (12:9). The dragon tried to devour a woman's newborn son, who would "rule all the nations" (12:4-5). But, failing at that, the dragon continued his attack on this King and his followers (12:17).

The prophet Isaiah sheds further light on Christ's birth in the midst of universal war: "People walking in darkness have seen a great light," and they can rejoice because "a child is born" who will be called "Prince of Peace" (Isa. 9:2-7). This prince's government and peace will have no end, because God has shattered the "yoke . . . of the oppressor" (9:4). When God's justice and righteousness prevail, then "every warrior's boot used in battle and every garment rolled in blood will be destined for burning, will be fuel for the fire" (9:5). This prophecy and many others about God's coming King and his kingdom of peace stand behind the angel's announcement that "in the town of David a Savior has been born to you; he is Christ the Lord" (Luke 2:11).

Luke continues to use biblical military images in the story of Jesus' birth and throughout his gospel. The phrase "great company of the heavenly host," for example, is more literally translated as "heavenly army" (2:13). The baby whose birth is announced by this army will grow up to do battle with the devil in the wilderness (4:1-13). But Jesus' warfare against Satan and his armies takes the unexpected form of healing, mercy, and, finally, death on a cross (see 4:31-35; 11:14-20; 22:51). As the apostle Paul puts it, "Having disarmed the powers and authorities, [God] made a public spectacle of them by the cross" (Col. 2:15). Further, the merciful and forgiving character of Jesus' kingdom is seen most vividly at the crucifixion, when Jesus promises paradise to the criminal who prays, "Jesus, remember me when you come into your kingdom" (Luke 23:42). By loving sinners even to the point of dying for them, Jesus ushers in a kingdom of reconciliation "by making peace through his blood, shed on a cross" (Col. 1:20). All these saving truths flow from Jesus' lowly birth. The cross looms over the manger as the Prince of Peace is born into a harsh world in which "there was no room" (Luke 2:7).

Peace Now through God's Favor

The kingdom of peace has invaded our world in the person of Jesus Christ and in the merciful lives of his followers. Until the final day, though, when the "God of peace" finally crushes Satan under our feet (see Rom. 16:20), Christ's kingdom will be at war with Satan's, and we will see terrible evidence of this spiritual warfare in the violence and sin that afflict our world. In the meantime, just as Jesus sent out "the Twelve" and the "seventy-two others," so he also sends us out to bear witness of God's kingdom by bringing the gospel of peace to every household and town we can reach (see Luke 9:1-6; 10:1-9).

As witnesses for God's kingdom of peace, we need to recognize what has been called the "upside-down" character of this kingdom. God's kingdom, as revealed in Christ's birth and ministry, turns many of our assumptions and values on their heads. Though it often looks small and weak, the kingdom of God will inevitably triumph. Just as the seeming failure of the cross led to the resurrection, so will our Christlike acts of mercy and healing lead to life and peace. As evidence we can consider that the small band who followed Jesus during his earthly career has grown, by the power of God's Spirit, into a worldwide fellowship. Such is the "upside-down" power of our King, who sends us out "like lambs among wolves" (10:3). A mere seventy-two witnesses to the Prince of Peace, acting with Jesus' authority, made "Satan fall like lightning from heaven" (10:18; see Rev. 12:9).

Additional Notes

2:1—Although the original Greek text lacks an explicit reference to the "Roman" world, the Greek word for "world" or "inhabited earth" was often used to refer to the Roman empire. By mentioning Caesar Augustus and Quirinius, Luke connects salvation history to world history (see also 3:1). This fits Luke's theme of proclaiming Jesus as Savior of the world.

2:7—The revealing truth that "there was no room" for the Savior of the world foreshadows the cross. Luke echoes this theme later when he records Jesus on his way to the cross saying, "The Son of Man has no place to lay his head" (9:58).

2:13—"a great company of the heavenly host" always stands ready to fight for God's cause on earth (see 2 Kings 6:16-17).

2:14—Older translations based on less accurate manuscripts spoke of peace on earth and "good will toward men" or to "men of goodwill." Through Christmas music, this older, less accurate translation still echoes in our minds. The "peace" Luke refers to is messianic peace (see Luke 1:79), which is not a political achievement or a reward for human merit but the gift of God to those on whom the Lord's "favor rests."

2:19—Twice Luke records that "Mary treasured up all these things and pondered them in her heart" (see also 2:51). In this way she was a model for disciples, who receive God's Word with "noble and good" hearts that persevere to produce a crop of obedience to God (8:15). Mary later had to relearn this lesson from Jesus (see 8:19-21).

GENERAL DISCUSSION

1. Compare the familiar song lyrics "peace on earth, good will to men," to the exact wording of Luke 2:14 (NIV). What difference does it make that God's peace comes to those "on whom his favor rests"?

2. On the basis of Isaiah 9:1-7 and many other prophecies, God's people Israel expected a king who would be descended from King David. What aspect of Jesus' birth "in the town of David" (Luke 2:11) would have surprised them?

3. Reflect on Luke 9:1-6 and 10:1-7, 17-20. In what ways is the spiritual war between God's kingdom and Satan's related to the wars and violence we see in our world? When, if ever, can we judge that a nation, group, or individual is completely on God's side or Satan's?

4. Discuss ways in which you and your church could say, "Peace to this house" (Luke 10:5), in a meaningful way. How could the gospel of peace bring the kingdom of God nearer to your hometown?

5. Do you have the joyful peace of knowing that your name is written in heaven (see Luke 10:20)? How can we have peace with God?

SMALL GROUP SESSION IDEAS

Opening (5-10 minutes)
Pray/Worship—Open your session with prayer, asking for the Lord's presence among you as you study about the peace of God's "upside-down" kingdom in the coming of Christ.

To add a worship element at this time, you may wish to sing together a familiar hymn such as "Joy to the World!" "Hark! The Herald Angels Sing," or "O Worship the King."

Share—Share with each other how you're doing on the goals you set in lesson 1. To lead into your study for this lesson, you may want to use this time also to review briefly what you learned in the previous lesson.

Focus—Ask yourselves the following focus question as you begin this session: *What does "the peace of God" mean to me?*

Growing (35-50 minutes)
Read (optional)—You may want to read Luke 2:1-20 together (and, if you have time, 10:1-7, 17-20, along with the study guide notes) before moving into your discussion time.

Discuss—Before choosing from among the following process questions for your discussion, you'll want to work through some of the General Discussion questions—especially 1, 2, and 5—focusing on the surprising peace of God's "upside-down" kingdom.

- When you think of peace, what's the first thing that comes to mind? How does that compare with "the peace of God" discussed in this lesson?

- Take a few moments to reflect on some "upside-down" kingdom experiences you may have had. Share one or two of them with your group, if you're comfortable doing so. In what ways did these experiences help you grow spiritually?

- In what ways can you make room in your life for Christ's kingdom and fight against Satan's? Challenge yourself to think in terms of your personal, family, social, local church, denominational, community, and national life.

Goalsetting (5 minutes)

Try working toward the following goal in the coming week:

• Here's how I'd like to apply what I've learned in this lesson about peace and God's kingdom:

Closing (5-10 minutes)

Preparing for Prayer—Share items that you'd like the others in your group to bring before God in prayer for you, both now and during the coming week. You may want to mention personal concerns and praises, the goals you've set so far in this Bible study, and so on.

Prayer—Close your meeting with prayer, thanking God for Christ's coming to usher in the kingdom of peace and to free us from the powers of sin and death. Everyone may join in with prayer concerns and praises.

When your group prayer is finished, you could add a worship element by reading together the following stanzas from *Our World Belongs to God* (st. 24-25):

God remembered his promise
to reconcile the world to himself;
he has come among us
in Jesus Christ,
the eternal Word made flesh.
He is the long-awaited Savior,
fully human and fully divine,
conceived by the Spirit of God
and born of the virgin Mary.

In the events of his earthly life—
his temptations and suffering,
his teaching and miracles,
his battles with demons and talks with sinners—
Jesus made present in deed and in word
the coming rule of God.

Wish each other God's peace as you part till your next meeting.

Group Study Project (Optional)

Some of you may be interested in pursuing the matter of discrepancies between the gospel accounts of Jesus' life and ministry, as well as possible errors regarding the date of Jesus' birth. Your group leader can summarize for you a brief discussion of this matter in the leader's guide notes for this session. If any of you wish to look further into the matter, you could consult I. Howard Marshall's *Commentary on Luke (New International Greek Testament Commentary)*, Raymond Brown's *The Birth of the Messiah*, and Joseph Fitzmyer's *The Gospel According to Luke*. Perhaps you could report on your findings when the group studies lesson 6 or lesson 8, in which the leader's guide material points out variations in Jesus' sermons and his teaching on prayer.

*How should we
pray for the
Spirit to work
in us?*

3

LUKE 3:15-23; 11:1, 9-13

Jesus and the Holy Spirit

In a Nutshell

The Spirit-empowered ministry of Jesus shows that the Holy Spirit is deeply concerned about bringing outsiders and underdogs—us!—into the people of God. So, in line with Jesus' ministry and mission, any emphasis on the Holy Spirit goes hand in hand with an emphasis on including outsiders. When we pray for the Holy Spirit as Jesus did, we will keep this double emphasis in mind, and the Spirit's gift of love will lead us to share Jesus' love and care for all people.

Luke 3:15-23

15The people were waiting expectantly and were all wondering in their hearts if John might possibly be the Christ. 16John answered them all, "I baptize you with water. But one more powerful than I will come, the thongs of whose sandals I am not worthy to untie. He will baptize you with the Holy Spirit and with fire. 17His winnowing fork is in his hand to clear his threshing floor and to gather the wheat into his barn, but he will burn up the chaff with unquenchable fire." 18And with many other words John exhorted the people and preached the good news to them.

19But when John rebuked Herod the tetrarch because of Herodias, his brother's wife, and all the other evil things he had done, 20Herod added this to them all: He locked John up in prison.

21When all the people were being baptized, Jesus was baptized too. And as he was praying, heaven was opened 22and the Holy Spirit descended on him in bodily form like a dove. And a voice came from heaven: "You are my Son, whom I love; with you I am well pleased."

23Now Jesus himself was about thirty years old when he began his ministry.

11:1, 9-13

1One day Jesus was praying in a certain place. When he finished, one of his disciples said to him, "Lord, teach us to pray, just as John taught his disciples." . . .

9"So I say to you: Ask and it will be given to you; seek and you will find; knock and the door will be opened to you. 10For everyone who asks receives; he who seeks finds; and to him who knocks, the door will be opened.

11"Which of you fathers, if your son asks for a fish, will give him a snake instead? 12Or if he asks for an egg, will give him a scorpion? 13If you then, though you are evil, know how to give good gifts to your children, how much more will your Father in heaven give the Holy Spirit to those who ask him!"

Additional reading: Luke 17:11-19; 19:1-10
See also Acts 2:1-12; 10:44-48

Controversy and Longing

At least since the time of Paul's letters to the Corinthians, the church has had many questions and disagreements about the work of the Holy Spirit (see 1 Cor. 12-14). As in Corinth, so today differing views on the gifts of the Spirit divide the body of Christ. Some Christians claim that their spiritual gifts make them superior to other Christians, while other believers feel they have insignificant gifts or no gift at all. In either case, believers sometimes expect the Spirit to boost them by means of an emotional high.

In some ways the longing for a keener sense of the Holy Spirit's activity in our lives is dangerous. It can be self-centered instead of Christ-centered and others-directed. But there is a proper and even necessary way of longing and praying for the Spirit's gifts and powers. The Spirit's work in Jesus' ministry points us to this "most excellent way" (1 Cor. 12:31).

The Spirit, Outsiders, and Underdogs

Alone among the evangelists, Luke notes that Jesus "was praying" at his baptism (Luke 3:21). As Jesus prays, the Holy Spirit descends on him "like a dove" (3:22). Empowered in this way (see 4:1, 14), Jesus "began his ministry" (3:23). And the Spirit-empowered ministry of Jesus reveals that the Holy Spirit has a special concern to bring outsiders and underdogs into the people of God.

Jesus announces this concern in the first of his sermons recorded by Luke (4:14-30; see also lesson 5). Quoting from Isaiah 61, Jesus announces, "The Spirit of the Lord is on me" (4:18). The Spirit anoints Jesus to bring good news in word and deed to the poor, the imprisoned, the sick, and the oppressed (4:18-19). As Jesus goes on to explain the Isaiah passage in detail, he indicates that the Spirit's promises extend even to Gentiles (4:25-27).

The gift of the Holy Spirit to the Gentiles is a major theme in the book of Acts. We won't explore that theme here, but you can examine it through another *Word Alive* study titled *Acts: Bursting the Boundaries* (1996, 2002). Our concern here is to see that the Spirit's mission to the Gentiles is foreshadowed in Jesus' mission to outsiders and underdogs. The Spirit and outreach go together.

As New Testament scholar Bastiaan Van Elderen points out, Luke places special emphasis on the theme that God's "redemption embraces people from all walks of life and with varied needs." Again and again Luke shares examples of Jesus' compassionate and healing love extended to tax collectors, sinners, the poor, the lowly, and the fallen. Further, Van Elderen notes, "Luke alone reports the cure of Mary Magdalene and certain other women (8:2), the anointing [by] the sinful woman (7:36-50), [the story of] Zacchaeus (19:1-10), [and] the promise to the penitent thief (23:43)." Jesus' teachings in Luke reinforce this theme. For example, only Luke records the parables of the lost coin and the lost son (15:8-24). Luke has thus sometimes been called "the Gospel of the Underdog." In addition to noting Luke's special emphasis on Jesus' concern for outsiders, Van Elderen notes Luke's "significant emphasis on the role of the Spirit in the life of Jesus and the church." Both Jesus' ministry and the mission of the church in Acts show that an emphasis on the Holy Spirit belongs together with an emphasis on including outsiders.

We can keep this dual emphasis in mind as we pray for the Holy Spirit. And when we ask for the Spirit, we can rest in Jesus' promise that our "Father in heaven [will] give the Holy Spirit to those who ask" (11:13). But our expectation may not be that the Spirit will elevate us above our fellow believers in terms of emotional highs or showy spiritual gifts. Instead we will expect to be inspired the way the Spirit inspired Jesus—that is, we will expect the Spirit to anoint us to reach out to those who are poor, imprisoned, sick, and oppressed—whether physically, spiritually, or both (see Matt. 25:31-46; Luke 5:27-32). The Spirit's greatest gift of love (see 1 Cor. 13) will compel us to share Jesus' compassion for outsiders and underdogs. As we carry on Jesus' mission in this way, we can be sure that the joy of the Spirit will be ours as well. After all, when the lost are found, it's time to celebrate (see Luke 15:7, 10, 24, 32).

Some Specific Directions

Hugh O'Driscoll suggests a way to give Jesus' baptism a very personal meaning for us: Imagine going into the waters of baptism with Jesus and coming out with a stronger sense of identification with him in his work. If we exercise our imaginations in this way, we can focus more faithfully on Jesus and find his life fusing into ours. When this happens, O'Driscoll says, "we have received the anointing of the Holy Spirit."

James Bryan Smith suggests two practical ways we can seek the Holy Spirit for this kind of anointing power. One way is to pray earnestly for the fruit of the Spirit as listed in Galatians 5:22-23. Seeking this fruit through sustained communion with God can lead to the growth of "love, joy, peace, patience," and so on in our lives. Second, we can examine the gifts of the Spirit listed in Romans 12, 1 Corinthians 12:7-30, and Ephesians 4:7-13. As we do so, we can ask God to give us a sense of what may be a neglected or underused gift in our lives.

We should add just one observation to the good suggestions O'Driscoll and Smith make. Seeking the Spirit is best done in the context of a group of people who are seeking to be conformed to Christ. We will never be led by the Spirit to increasing faith and commitment unless we recognize that the Holy Spirit is the Spirit of Christ and of the Christian community. The Spirit is always given "for the common good" (1 Cor. 12:7) and "to prepare God's people for works of service, so that the body of Christ may be built up" (Eph. 4:12).

Additional Notes

3:15—The impact John the Baptist made on people is clear in Luke's observation that people wondered "in their hearts if John might possibly be the Christ." John rightly denied this and bore witness to Jesus (Luke 3:16). Further, the impression John made on Jesus is revealed in Jesus' statements that John was "more than a prophet" and that "among those born of women there is no one greater than John" (7:26, 28). Recognizing the greatness of John makes the baptism of the Holy Spirit even more precious to us. Through the Spirit's life-giving power, even "the one who is least in the kingdom of God is greater than [John]" (7:28). For evidence that John's influence continued even after Jesus' death and resurrection, see Acts 19:1-7.

3:18—The inflexible demands of John's message could make us wonder how his preaching could be considered "good news." But like all of God's prophets, John did proclaim good news even as he preached judgment. John announced that God's redemption would come in the form of "one more powerful" (Luke 3:16), who would bring salvation. Luke 7:18-35 shows us how Jesus surprised even John the Baptist. But note also that Jesus did see John as a great prophet and that Jesus explained his own ministry in prophetic terms (7:33-35). (The works Jesus describes in Luke 7:22 fulfill promises God made in Isaiah 29 and 35. See also Luke 4:18

and Isaiah 61:1-2.) We can note further that Jesus, like John, also called people to bear fruit (Luke 6:43-45) and to repent or perish (13:1-9). Jesus was indeed gracious beyond John's expectations, but Jesus' grace is not a cheap denial of judgment or justice. Instead, it is an unexpected fulfillment of prophetic hopes for judgment and justice.

3:19—The Herod here is Herod Antipas, not to be confused with his father, Herod the Great, who died in 4 B.C. Herod Antipas ruled Galilee from 4 B.C. to A.D. 39.

3:22—Important Old Testament passages serving as background for Jesus' titles in this verse include Genesis 22:2; Psalm 2:7; and Isaiah 42:1. These, along with other Old Testament verses, tie together themes of sonship, kingship, and servanthood. The image of the suffering Servant especially foreshadows Christ's crucifixion for sinners (Isa. 52:13-53:12).

11:13—In this verse the original Greek text lacks the word "the" before "Holy Spirit." But Luke's strong theology of the Holy Spirit, especially as developed in the book of Acts, allows us to understand this phrase as it is translated here.

GENERAL DISCUSSION

1. Had you ever noticed the detail of Jesus' praying at his baptism? Why do you think Luke included this detail?

2. Is it easy or hard for you to believe that God calls you his daughter or son and that God loves you? Is it easy or hard to believe that God is well pleased with you? To what extent do circumstances affect your answer?

3. Does Luke 11:9-13 or any other biblical passage about prayer cause difficulty for you with respect to your own prayer experiences? Explain. How does Jesus' indication that we are asking for the Holy Spirit shed light on this?

4. Do you pray for the Holy Spirit? What do you expect from the Holy Spirit? What does this have to do with outsiders and underdogs?

5. What do you know of the charismatic movement? In what ways has it helped or hindered the church?

SMALL GROUP SESSION IDEAS

Opening (5-10 minutes)
Pray/Worship—Open with prayer, asking God to be present in each of you through the Holy Spirit as you study more about being like Christ, particularly in relation to the Spirit.

If you'd like to sing together, choose a song or two focusing on Christ, prayer, and the Holy Spirit, such as "Blessed Jesus, at Your Word" or "Lord, Listen to Your Children Praying."

Share—Share with each other how you're doing on the goals you've set in the previous sessions.

Focus—Ask yourselves the following focus question as you begin this session: *What do I know about the Holy Spirit's role in Jesus' mission?*

Growing (35-50 minutes)
Read (optional)—You may want to read Luke 3:15-23 and 11:1, 9-13 together (along with the study guide notes) before moving into your discussion time.

Discuss—Before choosing from among the following process questions for your discussion, you'll want to work through some of the General Discussion questions, especially noting questions 1, 3, 4, and 5.

• What have you learned in this lesson about the relationship between Christ, prayer, and the Holy Spirit? In what ways does it affect your outlook on prayer and your living for Christ as one of God's children?

- What spiritual gifts have you been given to use in living for Christ? What gifts are you aware of in your other group members? In other church members? (If you'd like to learn more about spiritual gifts, see the group study project suggestion at the end of this lesson.)

Goalsetting (5 minutes)

Try working on the following goal as a result of this lesson:

- I want to be more like Christ in my daily living, praying for the Spirit to fill me and use me. Here's what I'd like to work on, with the Spirit's help:

Closing (5-10 minutes)

Preparing for Prayer—Share items that you'd like the others in your group to bring before God in prayer for you, both now and during the coming week. You may want to mention personal concerns and praises, goals you've set so far in this Bible study, and so on.

Prayer—Close with prayer, thanking God for the Spirit's presence during this time of meeting and learning together. Ask the Spirit to move all of you to apply what you've learned in this session to your daily living. Everyone may join in with prayer concerns and praises.

After the prayer, you could read together the following stanzas from *Our World Belongs to God* (st. 30-33):

At Pentecost the Holy Spirit
was given to the church.
In pouring his Spirit on many peoples
God overcomes the divisions of Babel;
now people from every tongue, tribe, and nation
are gathered into the unity
of the body of Christ.

Jesus stays with us in the Spirit,
who renews our hearts,
moves us to faith,
leads us in the truth,
stands by us in our need,
and makes our obedience fresh and vibrant.

The Spirit thrusts
God's people into worldwide mission.
He impels young and old,
men and women,
to go next door and far away
into science and art,
media and marketplace
with the good news of God's grace.
The Spirit goes before them and with them,
convincing the world of sin
and pleading the cause of Christ.

The Spirit's gifts are here to stay
in rich variety—
fitting responses to timely needs.
We thankfully see each other
as gifted members of the fellowship
which delights in the creative Spirit's work.
He gives more than enough
to each believer
for God's praise and our neighbor's welfare.

Before parting, you may want to sing together "Spirit of the Living God" or another hymn asking for the Spirit's help and presence in your daily living.

Group Project/Study Goal (Optional)

Some or all of you may wish to learn more about your spiritual gifts and how to use them in living for Christ today. Your pastor or education leader may be able to schedule a workshop that you could attend. Several excellent studies on spiritual gifts are available, including the *Discover Your Gifts* workshop by CRC Publications. Call 1-800-333-8300 or visit *www.FaithAliveResources.org* for more information.

Jesus shows us how to endure temptation and testing.

4

LUKE 4:1-13

The Son in the Wilderness

In a Nutshell

When we recognize what the wilderness meant for Jesus, we learn that even in the midst of Satan's tempting, the Spirit was leading Jesus into a deeper understanding of what it meant to be the Son of God. By disciplining us through times of testing, God leads us to become more mature sons and daughters. Also, as we observe Jesus' lesson about his calling, we can better understand our own callings and the church's mission.

Luke 4:1-13

¹Jesus, full of the Holy Spirit, returned from the Jordan and was led by the Spirit in the desert, ²where for forty days he was tempted by the devil. He ate nothing during those days, and at the end of them he was hungry.

³The devil said to him, "If you are the Son of God, tell this stone to become bread."

⁴Jesus answered, "It is written: 'Man does not live on bread alone.'"

⁵The devil led him up to a high place and showed him in an instant all the kingdoms of the world. ⁶And he said to him, "I will give you all their authority and splendor, for it has been given to me, and I can give it to anyone I want to. ⁷So if you worship me, it will all be yours."

⁸Jesus answered, "It is written: 'Worship the Lord your God and serve him only.'"

⁹The devil led him to Jerusalem and had him stand on the highest point of the temple. "If you are the Son of God," he said, "throw yourself down from here. ¹⁰For it is written:

" 'He will command his angels concerning you
to guard you carefully;
11 they will lift you up in their hands,
so that you will not strike your
foot against a stone.'"

¹²Jesus answered, "It says: 'Do not put the Lord your God to the test.'"

¹³When the devil had finished all this tempting, he left him until an opportune time.

Additional reading: Luke 11:14-20; 17:20-25
See also Deuteronomy 8:1-10

A Dramatic Setting

Luke packs an immense amount of theological material and mystery into the very first sentence of the temptation story. Jesus is "full of the Holy Spirit" and is "led by the Spirit," but his destination is to be "tempted by the devil" (Luke 4:1-2). Those of us who have been taught by Jesus himself to pray, "Lead us not into temptation, but deliver us from evil" (Matt. 6:13, RSV), can well wonder why the Spirit would lead Jesus in such a way. One clue can be found in the word "desert" (also translated as "wilderness"—Luke 4:1, NRSV). Jesus' forty days in the wilderness remind us of the Israelites' forty years in the wilderness (see Num. 14:26-35; Deut. 8:3), Moses' fast during his encounter with God at Mount Sinai (Ex. 34:28), and Elijah's forty-day trek to "Horeb, the mountain of God" (Sinai), where God revealed himself to the prophet in "a gentle whisper" (1 Kings 19:8, 12). When we recognize what the wilderness meant for Jesus, we will better understand that even in the midst of Satan's tempting, the Spirit was leading Jesus into a deeper understanding of what it meant to be the Son of God. Also, by observing Jesus' lesson about his calling, we can better understand our own callings and the church's mission.

The Old Testament Background

Each time the devil challenged him, Jesus responded with a quotation from Scripture. And each time Jesus quoted Scripture, he quoted from the book of Deuteronomy—specifically, Deuteronomy 8:3; 6:13; and 6:16. These passages have to do with how God led the Israelites out of Egypt and through the wilderness in order to form them into the sort of people God was calling them to be. Deuteronomy 8:2-5 is especially clear on this point. This passage describes God's humbling of the Israelites in the wilderness and teaching them to live by God's word. It concludes with a parental image: "Know then in your heart that as a man disciplines his son, so the LORD your God disciplines you" (Deut. 8:5).

Jesus had learned this lesson by heart, and that's why he was able to believe God's announcement at his baptism—"You are my Son" (Luke 3:22)—even in the face of Satan's demand that he prove his identity: "If you are the Son of God . . ." (4:3, 9). While Satan would have Jesus define his sonship in terms of ease and self-exaltation, Jesus knew that God disciplines and humbles "those he loves" (Prov. 3:12; Heb. 12:6).

The very word that is translated here as "tempted" (*peirazo*) sheds more light on Jesus' wilderness experience. Although

Satan's intention clearly was to tempt Jesus, the Greek verb *peirazein* can also be translated as "test" or "try" in a positive sense. God tested both Abraham and the Israelites in this positive sense (see Gen. 22:2; Ex. 16:4; Deut. 8:2). God wanted the people to obey freely and lovingly, the way mature sons and daughters obey their parents. On the basis of this pattern, Jesus could know that even as Satan was tempting him in connection with his identity as the Son, God was testing Jesus by means of the Holy Spirit's leading him into a more profound relationship with the Father. As the author of Hebrews writes, "Although [Jesus] was a son, he learned obedience from what he suffered" (Heb. 5:8). Through this obedience, Jesus lived up to the announcement that the Father was "well pleased" with the beloved Son (Luke 3:22).

The Nature of Our Mission

Having seen God's intention in leading Jesus to be tested in the wilderness, we do well to give more attention to Satan's temptation of Jesus. Satan tempted Jesus to become a king without a cross. Having shown Jesus all the kingdoms of the world, the devil promised all the world's authority and splendor to Jesus on the condition that he worship him. The logic of this temptation is the logic of power. By seizing kingship instantaneously, Jesus could use his royal power to end hunger, abolish war, and command everyone to worship God. We might reason that these goals would be worth a compromise on Jesus' part.

But Jesus, of course, refused the devil's deal. He answered, "It is written: Worship the Lord your God and serve him only" (Luke 4:8). Jesus knew that God wanted his whole heart and soul and strength (Deut. 6:5) and that only through uncompromising obedience—even to "death on a cross"—could he be exalted by God as the ruler of all creation (see Phil. 2:5-11). As we noted in lesson 1, for Jesus, the way of God's kingdom is the way of the cross. The temptation story is a vivid example of the Christ-pattern (as noted in lesson 1), which disciples must take pains to learn.

The temptation story adds to our understanding of the cross by giving us the image of the wilderness. This image helps us believe that when we pass through confusing situations and difficult trials, God is still our Father. In fact, by disciplining us, God can draw us closer as more mature sons and daughters. Even though Satan is at work—and we can fight Satan and hate what he is doing—over and above Satan is God, leading us by the Holy Spirit into a more profound relationship, a relationship of free and loving obedience to the Lord.

Margaret Craven tells a touching version of a wilderness story in her novel *I Heard the Owl Call My Name*. A bishop, having learned that a young minister under his care has less than two years to live, wants those two years to be a time of profound learning for the young man. So the bishop says, "It leaves me no choice. I shall send him to my hardest parish." During his brief period of work among the Kwakiutl people in British Columbia, the young minister does indeed learn to love and to serve his neighbors in a Christlike way. His wilderness experience matures him as a child of God.

Not just individuals but also congregations and the whole church can use the image of the wilderness to gain understanding in how God is leading us.

Perhaps your church or small group is passing through a time of testing. Could the story of Jesus in the wilderness offer guidance? Ask yourselves this question: Is God's Word or Satan's allurement setting the tone for our mission?

Additional Notes

4:2—The word "tempted," or "tested" (*peirazein*), is clearly a key word for the whole lesson about Jesus' obedience. For Old Testament precedents of God's testing, see Genesis 22:2; Exodus 16:4; and Deuteronomy 8.2. For the development of the idea of Satan tempting God's people, compare 2 Samuel 24:1 to 1 Chronicles 21:1. While the first passage says, "The LORD . . . incited David . . . ," the latter passage, a later version of the earlier story, says that "Satan incited David" to take the disobedient census. This reveals both God's control over Satan and the development in Israel's thought regarding Satan's existence and activities (see also 2 Chron. 18:18-22; Job 1-2).

4:13—The "opportune time" for Satan's return to tempt Jesus would be the time near Jesus' crucifixion (see Luke 22:3, 31; John 12:27-31; 14:30). In the meantime, Jesus continued to battle demons (see Luke 4:33-34; 11:14-20).

11:20—Although Jesus refused to give skeptics a sign regarding his identity (see 11:16, 29), he acknowledged that his casting out of demons showed that "the kingdom of God has come" (11:20). Healing (see 11:14), which is born of Jesus' compassion and points forward to the new creation, is a legitimate sign of the kingdom. A miracle for the sake of impressing the crowd would be a satanic mockery of God's power (see 4:9-12).

GENERAL DISCUSSION

1. Think of an example or two in which you may have passed through a "wilderness time"—an experience in which you were tested by God and tempted by the devil at the same time. What happened? In what ways did the experience(s) affect your relationship with God?

2. Why would it have been wrong for Jesus to turn stones into bread?

3. Jesus did not compromise with Satan. But is compromise always wrong? When, if ever, can the church compromise with respect to worship and other issues we sometimes fight about?

4. In what ways do we sometimes put God to the test?

5. When might the church be tempted to equate success with God's blessing? Are success and faithfulness always at odds? Explain.

SMALL GROUP SESSION IDEAS

Opening (5-10 minutes)
Pray—Ask the Lord to help each of you grow in your ability to face testing and temptation as you reflect on Jesus' experience in the wilderness.

Share—Share with each other how you're doing on the goals you've set in previous sessions.

Focus—Ask yourselves the following focus question as you begin this session: *What do I do in times of testing?*

Growing (35-50 minutes)

Read (optional)—You may want try a reader's theater of Luke 4:1-13. If there's time, you may also wish to summarize the passages listed for additional reading (along with the study guide notes) before your discussion time.

Discuss—Before choosing from the following process questions for your discussion, you'll want to work through some of the General Discussion questions—especially 1, 2, and 4.

- Reflect on one or two times when you've been tested and tempted. What did you do? In what ways did God help? What did you learn from the experience(s)?

- Think of a time when you (may have) put God to the test. Compare and contrast the experience with a time when you stepped out obediently in faith. In what ways did each experience affect your relationship with God and with others?

- Describe one or two ways in which you see your church or group being tested and tempted today. In what ways do you see these things affecting the Master's mission? (Be sure to look for positive effects as well as negative ones.)

Goalsetting (5 minutes)

Try working on one of the following goals as a result of this lesson:

- Since I know Jesus withstood the devil's attacks, I need to ask my Lord's help in resisting the following temptations:

- I want to help my church or group in the following ways as we go through a period of testing and tempting:

Closing (5-10 minutes)

Preparing for Prayer—Share items that you'd like the others in your group to bring before God in prayer for you, both now and during the coming week.

Prayer—Close with prayer, thanking Jesus for being willing to be tempted and for resisting the devil's attacks for our sake. Everyone may join in with prayer concerns and praises. Encourage each other to withstand the devil's temptations in the coming week, with the help of Christ and the Holy Spirit.

*Who could
possibly hate
Jesus'
message?*

5

LUKE 4:14-30; 10:25-37

Listening to the Enemy

In a Nutshell

From the very beginning of his public work, Jesus sets the pattern for his whole ministry. An odd but revealing truth of God's "upside-down" kingdom is that the radical inclusiveness of Jesus' love breeds scandal that will lead to the cross. In this lesson we explore why the unexpectedly inclusive character of the kingdom offends religious insiders.

Luke 4:14-30

14Jesus returned to Galilee in the power of the Spirit, and news about him spread through the whole countryside. 15He taught in their synagogues, and everyone praised him.

16He went to Nazareth, where he had been brought up, and on the Sabbath day he went into the synagogue, as was his custom. And he stood up to read. 17The scroll of the prophet Isaiah was handed to him. Unrolling it, he found the place where it is written:

18 "The Spirit of the Lord is on me,
    because he has anointed me
    to preach good news to the poor.
He has sent me to proclaim
    freedom for the prisoners
    and recovery of sight for the blind,
to release the oppressed,
19   to proclaim the year of the Lord's
    favor."

20Then he rolled up the scroll, gave it back to the attendant and sat down. The eyes of everyone in the synagogue were fastened on him, 21and he began by saying to them, "Today this scripture is fulfilled in your hearing."

22All spoke well of him and were amazed at the gracious words that came from his lips. "Isn't this Joseph's son?" they asked.

23Jesus said to them, "Surely you will quote this proverb to me: 'Physician, heal yourself! Do here in your hometown what we have heard that you did in Capernaum.'"

24"I tell you the truth," he continued, "no prophet is accepted in his hometown. 25I assure you that there were many widows in Israel in Elijah's time, when the sky was shut for three and a half years and there was a severe famine throughout the land. 26Yet Elijah was not sent to any of them, but to a widow in Zarephath in the region of Sidon. 27And there were many in Israel with leprosy in the time of Elisha the prophet, yet not one of them was cleansed —only Naaman the Syrian."

28All the people in the synagogue were furious when they heard this. 29They got up, drove him out of the town, and took him to the brow of the hill on which the town was built, in order to throw him down the cliff. 30But he walked right through the crowd and went on his way.

10:25-37

25On one occasion an expert in the law stood up to test Jesus. "Teacher," he asked, "what must I do to inherit eternal life?"

26"What is written in the Law?" he replied. "How do you read it?"

27He answered: "'Love the Lord your God with all your heart and with all your soul and with all your strength and with all your mind'; and, 'Love your neighbor as yourself.'"

28"You have answered correctly," Jesus replied. "Do this and you will live."

29But he wanted to justify himself, so he asked Jesus, "And who is my neighbor?"

30In reply Jesus said: "A man was going down from Jerusalem to Jericho, when he fell into the hands of robbers. They stripped him of his clothes, beat him and went away, leaving him half dead. 31A priest happened to be going down the same road, and when he saw the man, he passed by on the other side. 32So too, a Levite, when he came to the place and saw him, passed by on the other side. 33But a Samaritan, as he traveled, came where the man was; and when he saw him, he took pity on him. 34He went to him and bandaged his wounds, pouring on oil and wine. Then he put the man on his own donkey, took him to an inn and took care of him. 35The next day he took out two silver coins and gave them to the innkeeper. 'Look after him,' he said, 'and when I return, I will reimburse you for any extra expense you may have.'

36"Which of these three do you think was a neighbor to the man who fell into the hands of robbers?"

37The expert in the law replied, "The one who had mercy on him."

Jesus told him, "Go and do likewise."

Additional reading: Luke 6:27-36; 9:46-50

The Crucifixion Foreshadowed

I once taught a group of young children a Bible lesson about the events leading up to Jesus' death. I told the children about Jesus' triumphant entry into Jerusalem. I explained that the people loved Jesus because he healed and loved them. "But then," I said, "some people arrested Jesus and nailed him to a cross, and Jesus died."

At that moment one little girl burst into tears. She was hearing the story of Jesus for the first time, and she, too, was learning to love him. Why, she wondered, would anyone want to hurt Jesus?

How would you answer a child who asked, "Why did people kill Jesus?" How would you answer that question from an adult? How do you answer it for yourself? Jesus was a healer and a teacher of love, yet people nailed him to a deadly instrument of torture. How could that be?

A children's Bible I own says this: "Bad men didn't like Jesus. They put him on a cross." How many adult believers hold to some version of this simplistic answer?

Jesus' inaugural sermon offers a biblical answer.

What Happened at Nazareth?

As the story begins, Jesus' ministry is off to a strong start. He is "in the power of the Spirit," and he has the praise of "everyone" (Luke 4:14-15). Even the sermon in his hometown synagogue starts well. Jesus reads from Isaiah 61, proclaims that this Scripture is being fulfilled, and all the people "[speak] well of him" (4:21).

Soon, however, the atmosphere changes. The congregation tries to throw Jesus off a cliff. What has happened? In a sermon titled "What Happened at Nazareth," James A. Sanders concludes that "Jesus interpreted Scripture . . . as a challenge to our limited view of truth, and we tried to lynch him."

Sanders points out that the congregation became "furious" (4:28) when Jesus interpreted Isaiah 61 by means of two other passages from the Old Testament. Jesus told the story of Elijah being sent to a widow in Zarephath and the story of Elisha cleansing a leper, Naaman the Syrian. Both this widow and this leper were Gentiles, non-Jews.

This infuriated the Nazarene congregation because Jesus had taken the promises of Isaiah 61 and applied them not to Jews but to Gentiles. Jesus was putting Gentiles, including the Romans, on equal footing with the Jews, who identified themselves as "the oppressed" (4:18) under Roman rule. Jesus, however, was saying that the Lord's favor applies equally to all kinds of people, whether Jew or Gentile, who live under the oppression of darkness—that is, sin and its effects in this world (4:19). So in their anger and misunderstanding the worshipers in Nazareth anticipated Good Friday by trying to kill Jesus right then and there.

Sanders says we make a fatal mistake if we judge the Nazarene congregation, or Jews in general, to be more narrow-minded than we are today. Rather, in order to read this story correctly, we must identify with the people who wanted to kill Jesus. We have to understand that God's freedom, God's strange way of extending favor to people we hate and to the ungrateful and wicked (see 6:27-36), will surprise and offend the people of God in all ages. In this story the Nazarene congregation represents the church. It portrays us, God's elect, whenever we think we possess Jesus instead of realizing that Jesus possesses us. Anytime we presume that we have Jesus all figured out, he will offend us, we will reject him, and he will walk "right through" us and go "on his way" (4:30).

An Alternative Response

There is, however, an alternative response: to recognize that Jesus is not just a healer and not just a teacher of love. Jesus is both of these and much more, but he is also a prophet (4:24). Because Jesus is a prophet, we can learn to expect him to offend us. We can expect him to proclaim God's judgment on the ways we try to impose limits on God's inclusive love.

In light of this judgment we can learn to listen for the message of Jesus in the voices of people who touch our sore spots and make us defensive or angry. Few of us today harbor resentment toward Romans, but, like the Nazarenes, we have plenty of people whom we do not like. Perhaps Jesus the prophet is speaking to us through just such people. Jesus may be speaking to us through someone on the other side of the political or theological spectrum. He may be speaking to us through someone in our congregation or denomination whom we cannot stand. Jesus may not be calling us to agree with our enemies, but he does call us to love them and to change our minds in the sense of, at the very least, having the humility to listen to them more attentively, pray for them more fervently, and treat them with Christlike love.

We may find that we resent our enemies because, if we admit any truth to what they say, we'll have to repent of hatred and change our ways. Through such repentance, however, Jesus can call us to new life (5:31-32). Jesus can call us to this repentance whenever we realize that the people who wanted to kill him were not any more "bad" than we are; they were the people who gathered for worship that Sabbath day in Nazareth just as we gather in church on Sundays. In other words, they were people much like us.

Repentance in the Form of Neighbor Love

Jesus' parable of the good Samaritan (10:25-37) helps us to see how we can put this repentance into action in the form of neighbor love. This rich parable speaks to us in many ways, but its main message is a critique of racial and religious boundaries that imprison our love in chains of pride. As scholar-preacher Frederick Neumann states in a sermon on this parable, "Jesus did not argue with religious or racial discriminators. . . . With the example of the Samaritan mongrel who obeyed the word of God's love in contradistinction to the purebread orthodox who disobeyed it, he exploded the religious and racial pride of his people." When we let Jesus destroy our pride in a similar way, we open our eyes to the way God loves the outsiders and enemies we are tempted to exclude.

Additional Notes

4:16—Note that "on the Sabbath day" Jesus "went into the synagogue, as was his custom." This reminds us of how Jewish Jesus was. He did not repudiate the Jewish idea of Sabbath, though he did reinterpret it (see Luke 6:1-9).

4:19—The "year of the Lord's favor" refers specifically to the year of Jubilee, described in Leviticus 25, in which debts were to be forgiven and slaves set free. The word translated here as "favor" (*dektos*) recurs in 4:24, when Jesus says no prophet is *dektos*, or "accepted," in one's hometown. These references to justice and to prophets remind us that the kingdom of God has concrete social and political implications.

10:30, 34—The references to both Jericho and healing oil refer back to the story about Jews and Samaritans in 2 Chronicles 28:15.

10:31—The "priest" would have defiled himself if he touched a dead body, which this beaten man may have appeared to be (see Lev. 21:1-3). Being defiled in this way would have brought uncleanness and guilt upon him, restricted his activities severely, and called for him to make ritual atonement (see 5:2-6).

10:33—The verb for "took pity" is a strong one. It has to do with a gut-level movement of compassion. Jesus felt this way when he saw the widow of Nain mourning her only son. The same verb is used in the passage describing that event (Luke 7:13).

10:37—The Samaritan's act of "mercy" fulfills Micah 6:8: "What does the LORD require of you? To act justly and to love mercy and to walk humbly with your God." The Samaritan's mercy also breaks down racial and religious barriers. Jesus' healing of a Samaritan leper (Luke 17:11-19) similarly combined compassion and social inclusion.

GENERAL DISCUSSION

1. Were the people who wanted to kill Jesus bad? Is there hope for people who become "furious" (Luke 4:28) with Jesus?

2. Think about what it means that Jesus is a prophet. What does Jesus mean by saying, "No prophet is accepted in his hometown" (Luke 4:24)?

3. Are Jews more narrow-minded than Gentile Christians? Are there groups of people you tend to dislike or even hate? Explain.

4. Try to retell the parable of the good Samaritan by using contemporary labels for people. Do you have any sympathy for the priest and the Levite in Jesus' parable? Explain. What's Jesus' point in telling this parable?

SMALL GROUP SESSION IDEAS

Opening (5-10 minutes)

Pray—Open with prayer, thanking God for bringing you together again for another lesson from Luke, and asking for the Spirit's guidance as you consider why Jesus was rejected at Nazareth.

Share—Share with each other how you're doing on the goals you've set in previous sessions. Now may also be a good time to check on the progress or planning of any group projects you may have chosen to do.

Focus—Ask yourselves the following focus question as you begin this session: *What prejudices might I have against some groups or types of people?*

Growing (35-50 minutes)

Read (optional)—You may want to read together Luke 4:14-30 and 10:25-37, with each person taking a paragraph. You may also want to review the study guide notes before beginning your discussion time.

Discuss—Before choosing from the following process questions for your discussion, you'll want to work through some of the General Discussion questions—especially 1, 3, and 4.

- What do you think of the people who wanted to kill Jesus? In what ways are you like them?

- Think of someone you know (or know of) who broke through a barrier of prejudice in his or her life. In what ways do you see this event building up the body of Christ?

- Look back on your own experiences, and try to come up with one or two examples that would show how any of us might fall into the trap of "listening to the enemy" while trying to be a Christian. (Recall the priest and the Levite in Jesus' parable—Luke 10:25-37.) What difference do you see between *trying* to be a Christian and *being* one?

Goalsetting (5 minutes)
Try working on the following goal as a result of this lesson:

- With Jesus' help, I want to work on these areas in my life with respect to loving my neighbors:

Closing (5-10 minutes)
Preparing for Prayer—Share items that you'd like the others in your group to bring before God in prayer for you, both now and during the coming week.

Prayer—Close with prayer, thanking Jesus for teaching us to love our neighbors, and asking the Spirit's help in showing God's love to everyone around us. All of you may join in with prayer concerns and praises.

Before parting, you may wish to sing together "They'll Know We Are Christians by Our Love" or another song that reminds us of our oneness and our love in Christ.

*Why are the
poor more
likely to follow
Jesus?*

6

LUKE 6:17-36

A Kingdom of Blessing and Woe

In a Nutshell

In his Sermon on the Plain, Jesus draws a strong contrast between people who are poor and those who are rich. In this lesson there are at least two good reasons to look squarely at money issues. First, they're a major theme for Luke. And, second, we need to think honestly about Jesus' teachings on wealth and poverty. Looking at how we handle money is one revealing way to examine how much we truly trust God and whether we truly love our neighbors.

Luke 6:17-36

17He went down with them and stood on a level place. A large crowd of his disciples was there and a great number of people from all over Judea, from Jerusalem, and from the coast of Tyre and Sidon, 18who had come to hear him and to be healed of their diseases. Those troubled by evil spirits were cured, 19and the people all tried to touch him, because power was coming from him and healing them all.

20Looking at his disciples, he said:

"Blessed are you who are poor,
for yours is the kingdom of God.
21 Blessed are you who hunger now,
for you will be satisfied.
Blessed are you who weep now,
for you will laugh.
22 Blessed are you when men hate you,
when they exclude you and
insult you

and reject your name as evil,
because of the Son of Man.

23"Rejoice in that day and leap for joy, because great is your reward in heaven. For that is how their fathers treated the prophets.

24 "But woe to you who are rich,
for you have already received
your comfort.
25 Woe to you who are well fed now,
for you will go hungry.
Woe to you who laugh now,
for you will mourn and weep.
26 Woe to you when all men speak
well of you,
for that is how their fathers
treated the false prophets.

27"But I tell you who hear me: Love your enemies, do good to those who hate you, 28bless those who curse you, pray for those who mistreat you. ²⁹If someone strikes you on one cheek, turn to him the other also. If someone takes your cloak, do not stop him from taking your tunic. ³⁰Give to everyone who asks you, and if anyone takes what belongs to you, do not demand it back. ³¹Do to others as you would have them do to you.

³²"If you love those who love you, what credit is that to you? Even 'sinners' love those who love them. ³³And if you do good to those who are good to you, what credit is that to you? Even 'sinners' do that. ³⁴And if you lend to those from whom you expect repayment, what credit is that to you? Even 'sinners' lend to 'sinners,' expecting to be repaid in full. ³⁵But love your enemies, do good to them, and lend to them without expecting to get anything back. Then your reward will be great, and you will be sons of the Most High, because he is kind to the ungrateful and wicked. ³⁶Be merciful, just as your Father is merciful."

Additional reading: Luke 12:13-34; 16:1-31; 18:18-30

Tevye's Objection

Jesus' words "Blessed are you who are poor" (Luke 6:20) and "Woe to you who are rich" (6:24) almost certainly shocked his contemporaries (see 18:25-26). These words also shock us, whether we are encountering them for the first time or considering them in a fresh way. This shock can lead either to sadness and vague feelings of guilt (see 18:23) or to gladness and wholehearted obedience. Allowing our God-given common sense to have its say helps us move toward the latter response.

The character Tevye in the musical *Fiddler on the Roof* expresses our common-sense objection to Jesus' statements about poverty and riches. In the midst of an argument Tevye is having with God about his own financial distress, he says, "I know that to be poor is no disgrace. On the other hand, it's no great honor either."

To me, Tevye makes a lot of sense. In my—admittedly limited—experience, poor people are no better or worse than rich people. And the Bible would seem to support my observations. Abraham, to whose side poor Lazarus goes in Jesus' parable in Luke 16:22, was rich. And according to Jeremiah, the poor people in Jerusalem were no more honest and upright than anyone else in the city (Jer. 5:1-5). Why then does Jesus say, "Blessed are you who are poor," and, "Woe to you who are rich"?

The Poor and the Kingdom

We can begin to answer this by noting who has gathered around Jesus to hear his words. According to Luke, these were people who had come to be healed; they were troubled by diseases and evil spirits, and they were trying to touch Jesus in order to receive his power (Luke 6:18-19). In other words, these were people who were in need. Many of them were probably economically poor. They knew they were needy, and they knew they needed help. These people were like those whom Jesus had described earlier as being most likely to become his disciples. After the tax-collector Levi "left everything" to follow Jesus (5:28), the respectable religious leaders objected to the company Jesus was keeping. Jesus replied, "It is not the healthy who need a doctor, but the sick. I have not come to call the righteous, but sinners to repentance" (5:31-32).

Just as people who know they are sick sinners are more likely to follow Jesus as the Savior, so people who know they are poor are more likely to follow Jesus as the proclaimer of God's kingdom. In the kingdom of God the hungry are satisfied, the sorrowing are comforted, and the hated and excluded are united with Christ (6:21-22). Who will listen more eagerly to Jesus as he promises such a kingdom—people who know they have nothing to lose and much to gain, or people who think they have a lot to lose and nothing to gain? (The sad irony here is that what the rich think they stand to lose is *nothing* compared to what they stand to gain in Christ.)

Jesus blesses the poor *in relation to* the kingdom of God. He doesn't teach that poverty is good in itself or that his followers should promote poverty. He does, however, alert us to the truth that poor people have important advantages with respect to God's kingdom. As Philip Yancey puts it, "Through no choice of their own—[for] they may urgently wish otherwise— poor people find themselves in a posture that befits the grace of God. In their state of neediness, dependence, and dissatisfaction with life, they may welcome God's free gift of love."

On the other hand, Jesus warns those who have all they need and more because it is hard "for the rich to enter the kingdom of God" (18:24). This is true because we who are rich are more likely to be "choked by life's worries, riches, and pleasures" in a way that stunts our desire for God's kingdom (8:14). Out of love, therefore, Jesus warns us, "Remember Lot's wife! Whoever tries to keep his life will lose it, and whoever loses his life will preserve it" (17:32-33). Jesus wants us to be ready to leave everything to follow him—not because he wants us to be miserable but because our "Father has been pleased to give [us] the kingdom" (12:32). If we seek this kingdom first, Jesus promises, everything else will be given to us as well (12:31; Matt. 6:33).

Economic Platform or Kingdom Proclamation?

Someone in a crowd once said to Jesus, "Teacher, tell my brother to divide the inheritance with me." But Jesus replied, "Man, who appointed me a judge or an arbiter between you?" Jesus then went on to issue a general warning against greed (12:13-15).

That story helps us remember that Jesus was not appointed as a political economist. If Jesus had set out a detailed blueprint for economic reform in first-century Palestine, his teachings about poverty and wealth would be almost useless to us. As it is, Jesus gave us more lasting teachings, such as "one's life does not consist in the abundance of possessions" (12:15, NRSV). And beyond this Jesus inspires us to be "rich toward God" (12:21).

In Luke 16:1-9 Jesus tells what is often called the parable of the shrewd manager. In this memorable but perplexing story, a dishonest manager, about to be fired, cheats his employer so that after he loses his job, people will welcome him into their homes (16:4). The twist to this story is that "the master commended the dishonest manager because he had acted shrewdly" (16:8). Jesus, while warning against dishonesty and slavery to money (16:10-15), does seem to praise shrewdness (16:8-9). Could this offer a clue for how disciples can "use worldly wealth" (16:9)?

In *The Kingdom Equation* (CRC Publications, 1990) John Timmer suggests that to understand this parable, we need to recognize that the manager is commended for his resourcefulness in a time of dire crisis. "Just as the manager, confronted by a life-threatening situation, considers his options and chooses the one that offers the best possible future," writes Timmer, "so we ought to make an appropriate response to the crisis in which Jesus' preaching of the kingdom of God places us." Jesus' words in Luke 16:9 help us to apply this parable as follows, suggests Timmer: "If the dishonest manager provides for his future by an improper use of possessions, how much more should Christians, through proper use of money, provide for their eternal future. Blessed are those who share their wealth with the poor, for theirs is the kingdom of heaven." (Compare with Luke 6:35.)

In addition, consider that most, if not all, kingdom causes, including those that try to bring economic aid and justice to the poor, need managers who know how to generate and use money effectively. These causes need people who fit the paraphrase of this parable as told by Eugene Peterson in *The Message:* streetwise people, says Jesus, "are on constant alert, looking for angles, surviving by their wits. I want you to be smart in the same way—but for what is *right*." Perhaps this perspective can guide those of us who feel called not to sell everything we have in order to follow Jesus but to be ready to dedicate our whole lives to the kingdom of God. We can be smart with our money not for selfish purposes but for God's purposes in this world.

Additional Notes

6:20—To be "blessed" traditionally meant to enjoy happiness and well-being as bestowed by God (see Ps. 127:3-5). Jesus makes the word paradoxical by pairing it with being poor, hungry, and so on. Those who are maladjusted to the world in its present form are "blessed" in that they eagerly await the good things of the coming "kingdom of God." Jesus, then, ties blessedness to our hope for the last things—that is, the return of Christ and the consummation of the kingdom.

The Old Testament background for the term "the poor" is the term *anawim,* which refers to people who, out of need, "called on God for help and received it," observes I. Howard Marshall. The term has profound economic implications, but should not be reduced to a sheerly economic condition.

6:24—The idea of judgment is included in the word "woe," but so is the idea of pity and grief.

6:29—"Turn to him the other [cheek]." Joseph Fitzmyer observes that the cluster of commands surrounding this one has to do with cutting "through the old principle of retaliation."

6:31—The so-called "golden rule"—"Do to others as you would have them do to you"—has both Old Testament and pagan antecedents (see Lev. 19:18). Often, but not always, these other versions of the "golden rule" were put in more negative forms than Jesus' commandment was.

GENERAL DISCUSSION

1. People often speak of being blessed, and we easily pray for God's blessing. What does it mean to be blessed by God?

2. Jesus tells us to rejoice if we suffer rejection because of him (Luke 6:22-23). Is this command beyond human capacity? In what ways is the Sermon on the Plain (see also the Sermon on the Mount—Matt. 5-7) beyond human ability? In what ways not?

3. Jesus refused to serve as a judge or arbiter (Luke 12:14-15). When, however, might Christians appeal to judges to settle matters like inheritance claims?

4. Compare the "certain ruler" in Luke 18:18 to the stories of Levi (5:27-32) and Zacchaeus (19:1-10). What do you make of the variety of responses these people gave to Jesus? Which of these examples serves as a model for you?

5. Let's say a couple has done so well in the construction business that they can afford to retire at age 50. Should they retire and work for a relief organization? Or should they continue to make money in order to donate it and also to provide employment for people?

SMALL GROUP SESSION IDEAS

Opening (5-10 minutes)

Pray/Worship—Open your meeting with prayer, asking the Lord to help you as you study about how the money we have can affect our outlook on the kingdom of God.

To include a worship element, you might read a meditation that focuses on poverty, riches, and kingdom living, and you could sing "Seek Ye First the Kingdom" or another song focusing on Christ's kingdom teaching.

Share—Share with each other how you're doing on the goals you've set in previous sessions. Now (or perhaps in lesson 8) may be a good time for a brief discussion on the synoptic challenge, if any of you have chosen to study that topic (see the group project suggested in lesson 2).

Focus—Keep in mind the following question as you work through this session: *To what extent do I feel I need God?*

Growing (35-50 minutes)
Read (optional)—You may want to read Luke 6:17-36 together and review the passages for additional reading (as well as the study guide notes) before moving into your discussion time.

Discuss—Choose from among the following process questions after working through some of the General Discussion questions—especially questions 1, 4, and 5.

- In this lesson, what have you learned about "the poor"? About "the rich"? About the kingdom of God?

- Think of a Christian you know (or know of) who is economically poor. In what ways does this person show that he or she is "blessed"—focused on God and the kingdom?

- Think of a Christian you know (or know of) who is wealthy. In what ways is this person Christlike to those who are poor? To others?

- Discuss whether you think it's easier to be a Christian who is wealthy or one who is poor.

Goalsetting (5 minutes)
Try working on the following goal as a result of this lesson:

- Here's what I want to do, with the Spirit's help, to focus more on kingdom living:

Closing (5-10 minutes)
Preparing for Prayer—Share items that you'd like the others in your group to bring before God in prayer for you, both now and during the coming week.

Prayer—Close with prayer, thanking God for wanting to give us the kingdom and for teaching us how to live in it. Everyone may join in with prayer concerns and praises.

Before parting, you may want to sing a closing song that focuses on serving one another for Christ's sake, such as "The Servant Song."

Group Project/Study Goal (Optional)

Some or all of you may wish to learn more about using the money God gives us. Your pastor or education committee may be able to help you set up a stewardship workshop, perhaps for all church members. We recommend the following resources: *Faith and Finances: Helping People Manage Their Money*, *The Joy of Generosity: Stewardship Resources for Your Church*, *Becoming a Firstfruits Congregation: A Stewardship Guide for Church Leaders*, and more. Call Faith Alive Christian Resources at 1-800-333-8300 or visit *www.FaithAliveResources.org* for more information.

*Are we willing
to "give up
everything" to
follow Jesus?*

7

The Reward of Discipleship

In a Nutshell

Discipleship will cost us, but, as Jesus indicates, taking up our crosses is the only way to follow him. Following Jesus, though, comes with a reward that far outweighs any cost we might suffer along the way. With no embarrassment whatsoever—because he's telling the truth—Jesus claims that sharing his way of life is better than gaining "the whole world" (Luke 9:25; see 4:5-8).

Luke 9:18-27

18Once when Jesus was praying in private and his disciples were with him, he asked them, "Who do the crowds say I am?"

19They replied, "Some say John the Baptist; others say Elijah; and still others, that one of the prophets of long ago has come back to life."

20"But what about you?" he asked. "Who do you say I am?"

Peter answered, "The Christ of God."

21Jesus strictly warned them not to tell this to anyone. 22And he said, "The Son of Man must suffer many things and be rejected by the elders, chief priests and teachers of the law, and he must be killed and on the third day be raised to life."

23Then he said to them all: "If anyone would come after me, he must deny himself and take up his cross daily and follow me. 24For whoever wants to save his life will lose it, but whoever loses his life for me will save it. 25What good is it for a man to gain the whole world, and yet lose or forfeit his very self? 26If anyone is ashamed of me and my words, the Son of Man will be ashamed of him when he comes in his glory and in the glory of the Father and of the holy angels. 27I tell you the truth, some who are standing here will not taste death before they see the kingdom of God."

14:25-35

25Large crowds were traveling with Jesus, and turning to them he said: 26"If anyone comes to me and does not hate his father and mother, his wife and children, his brothers and sisters—yes, even his own life—he cannot be my disciple. 27And anyone who does not carry his cross and follow me cannot be my disciple.

28"Suppose one of you wants to build a tower. Will he not first sit down and estimate the cost to see if he has enough money to complete it? 29For if he lays the foundation and is not able to finish it, everyone who sees it will ridicule him,

55

30saying, 'This fellow began to build and was not able to finish.'

31"Or suppose a king is about to go to war against another king. Will he not first sit down and consider whether he is able with ten thousand men to oppose the one coming against him with twenty thousand? 32If he is not able, he will send a delegation while the other is still a long way off and will ask for terms of peace. 33In the same way, any of you who does not give up everything he has cannot be my disciple.

34"Salt is good, but if it loses its saltiness, how can it be made salty again? 35It is fit neither for the soil nor for the manure pile; it is thrown out.

"He who has ears to hear, let him hear."

Additional reading: Luke 22:24-30

A Siren Call
A great theologian and preacher named Helmut Thielicke compares Jesus' description of discipleship to the alarming sound of a siren, which one uses "to call attention to danger." Ordinarily Jesus attracts us with his combination of compassion and winsomeness. In Luke 9 and 14, however, Jesus seems to repel us. In Luke 9, having described the gruesome way in which he will die, Jesus insists that his disciples must die in a similar way by taking up their crosses daily and following him (9:22-23). In Luke 14 Jesus says this cross-bearing way of discipleship will express itself in hating the people closest to us and even our own lives. A parallel passage indicates that, when Jesus made similar statements on another occasion, "many of his disciples said, 'This is a hard teaching. Who can accept it?'" (John 6:60). What shall we make of these siren statements?

The Cross, the Life, and the Glory
The first thing we should do is honestly acknowledge what Dietrich Bonhoeffer called "the cost of discipleship." We must repudiate any idea that because God's grace is free, it is also "cheap," as Bonhoeffer puts it. We must, says Bonhoeffer, "attempt to recover a true understanding of the mutual relation between grace and discipleship." One interesting and biblical way to do this is to acknowledge not only the cost but also the reward of discipleship.

Jesus indicates that, while following him will cost us everything—including our very lives—it is also the only way for us to save our lives. Having called us to follow him by bearing our crosses—that is, to serve God and love our neighbors so passionately that we sacrifice ourselves and suffer for others—Jesus goes on to describe the reward this action brings. He explains, "Whoever wants to save his life will lose it, but whoever loses his life for me will save it" (9:24). Far from being embarrassed to offer a reward to his followers, Jesus claims that sharing his way of life is better than gaining "the whole world" (9:25).

Jesus roots this promise partly in the future when he refers to his return "in his glory and in the glory of the Father and of the holy angels" (9:26). But the rewards of discipleship also apply to this present life, for he said, "Some who are standing here will not taste death before they see the kingdom of God" (9:27). The kingdom of God is most assuredly coming because, in order to defeat Satan, Jesus is willing to suffer and die before being raised to life. Therefore, when we "estimate the cost" of discipleship (see 14:28), we do so with the assurance that our King has more than enough power to overcome the false king of this world (see 14:31-32). So it's a matter of sanctified common sense for us to be willing to "give up everything" to be Jesus' disciples (14:33).

The Dead-End Alternative

Frederick Buechner, in his autobiography *The Sacred Journey*, helps us to put flesh on Jesus' call to discipleship by describing a key event in his own conversion to Christ. One evening, Buechner had arranged to have dinner with his widowed mother. The evening promised to be quiet but delightful, but then the phone rang. A friend of Buechner's asked to speak to him. Before the friend could get out many words, he began to weep. Then he managed to explain that his mother, father, and sister had been in a car accident and might not survive. He was at the airport waiting to fly out to be with them. Desperate for comfort, he asked Buechner to wait with him.

Buechner confesses that he was afraid to go to his friend and share his painful sorrow. In a stalling tactic, he asked his friend to call back after he'd had time to take care of a few things. A few moments later, however, the unexpected reaction of his mother helped Buechner begin to follow the way of the cross.

When he explained the phone call to his mother, she said his friend's request was absurd. He was behaving like a child and had no business imposing on a friend that way. Buechner, who had been thinking similar thoughts himself, was revolted to hear these words from his mother's lips. He resolved that when his friend called again, he would offer to come immediately. Upon further reflection, he also began to understand that to live for yourself "is little by little to cease to live in any sense that really matters." In other words, he caught a glimpse of the truth in Jesus' saying "Whoever wants to save his life will lose it, but whoever loses his life for me will save it" (9:24).

Choose Life

When Jesus demands that we pick up our crosses, therefore, he is actually repeating God's appeal as recorded in Deuteronomy 30:19: "This day I call heaven and earth as witnesses against you that I have set before you life and death, blessings and curses. Now choose life. . . ." Jesus' own brave and beautiful death for his friends, sinners whom he loved, illustrates the principle of the seed: "Unless a kernel of wheat falls to the ground and dies, it remains only a single seed. But if it dies, it produces many seeds" (John 12:24). This principle of losing life for the sake of gaining it runs throughout the Scriptures. As C. S. Lewis notes at the end of *Mere Christianity,* this principle also "runs through all life from top to bottom. . . . Look for yourself and you will find in the long run only hatred, loneliness, despair, rage, ruin, and decay. But look for Christ and you will find Him, and with Him everything else thrown in."

Additional Notes

9:18—Once again (as in the account of Jesus' baptism) Luke is the only one among the evangelists who records that Jesus "was praying" at this critical juncture in his ministry.

9:21—We can cite at least three reasons why Jesus tells the disciples "not to tell . . . anyone" his identity: the time had not yet come to make his claims in a way that would lead to his death; the crowds would not understand what he meant by "Christ"; the disciples also did not know yet what Jesus meant by "Christ."

9:22—For the importance of the word "must" in this verse, see the note on Luke 24:26 in lesson 1.

9:23—Luke is the only gospel writer who presents Jesus as saying his disciples must pick up their crosses "daily." Perhaps because he was well aware that Jesus' return was delayed beyond what many early Christians expected, Luke stresses a daily discipleship that can endure as long as God's timing demands.

9:24—The word for "life" here, *psyche,* can also be translated as "soul." The "soul" that we are called to lose for Jesus' sake is a person's essence or essential self.

9:27—"See[ing] the kingdom of God" before tasting death has to do with the "already" presence of the kingdom in the life, death, resurrection, and continuing work of the ascended Jesus (see the section "Kingdom Fulfillment Now" in lesson 5 of this leader's guide). Jesus' disciples saw the kingdom revealed in his death and resurrection and in the outpouring of the Holy Spirit at Pentecost. In all these events, Jesus was inaugurating the long-promised kingdom of God.

GENERAL DISCUSSION

1. Note that Peter represented the disciples in confessing that Jesus is "the Christ of God" (Luke 9:20). How does Peter's life after this point, including his denials of Jesus, further represent the way of discipleship? (See Luke 22:54-62; John 21:15-23; Acts 2:14-40; 3:1-4:35; 10:1-11:18; 12:1-19; 15:7-11.)

2. Spend some time reflecting on Dietrich Bonhoeffer's terms "cheap grace" and "the cost of discipleship." Has Bonhoeffer's message gotten through to the church? Has it gotten through to you?

3. Can you tell any stories from your life or from the lives of others that illustrate the rewards of discipleship? Share one or two examples, if you're comfortable doing so.

4. What does it mean to "hate" the members of our families and even our own lives (Luke 14:26)?

5. What does it mean to "give up everything" in order to be Jesus' disciple (Luke 14:33)?

SMALL GROUP SESSION IDEAS

Opening (5-10 minutes)

Pray/Worship—Open your meeting with prayer, asking Jesus to guide you by his Spirit as you learn about being disciples.

You may also wish to read and reflect on the following stanza from *Our World Belongs to God* (st. 45):

> The rule of Jesus Christ covers
>> the whole world.
> To follow this Lord is
> to serve him everywhere,
> without fitting in,
> as light in the darkness,
> as salt in a spoiling world.

Then sing together, if you like, a song about following and serving Jesus, such as "Lead On, O King Eternal" or "If You but Trust in God to Guide You."

Share—Share with each other how you're doing on the goals you've set in previous sessions.

Focus—Keep in mind the following question as you work through this session: *How important is discipleship to me?*

Growing (35-50 minutes)

Read (optional)—You may want to read or review together the Scripture passages and the study guide notes before moving into your discussion time.

Discuss—You'll want to work through most or all of the General Discussion questions—especially questions 1, 2, and 3—before choosing from the following process questions.

- In what ways is your life as a follower of Jesus similar to Peter's life? What aspects of his life encourage you and inspire you to follow Jesus more closely?

- What goes through your mind when you think about giving over your whole life to God? In what ways, if any, are you afraid of spiritual success or failure?

Goalsetting (5 minutes)

Try working on the following goal as a result of this lesson:

- Here's what I need to work on to be a more faithful disciple of my Lord and Savior:

Closing (5-10 minutes)

Preparing for Prayer—Share items that you'd like the others in your group to bring before God in prayer for you, both now and during the coming week.

Then, before closing in prayer, you may wish to read together Jesus' words in John 13:34-35 about being his disciples.

Prayer—Ask God to help each one of you live in love and obedience as Jesus' disciples. Everyone may join in with prayer concerns and praises. Then, as you part, wish each other the power and presence of Christ's Spirit as you go out to live as his disciples.

EVALUATIONS

Please fill out the evaluation form at the back of this study guide. Your answers and suggestions help us as we develop other studies in the *Word Alive* series. Thank you!

Please mail your evaluation to

Word Alive / Luke (Part One)
Faith Alive Christian Resources
2850 Kalamazoo Ave. SE
Grand Rapids, MI 49560

Evaluation

Background

Size of group:
- [ ] fewer than 5 persons
- [ ] 5-10
- [ ] 10-15
- [ ] more than 15

Age of participants:
- [ ] 20-30
- [ ] 31-45
- [ ] 46-60
- [ ] 61-75 or above

Length of group sessions:
- [ ] under 60 minutes
- [ ] 60-75 minutes
- [ ] 75-90 minutes
- [ ] 90-120 minutes or more

Please check items that describe you:
- [ ] male
- [ ] female
- [ ] ordained or professional church staff person
- [ ] elder or deacon
- [ ] professional teacher
- [ ] church school or catechism teacher (three or more years' experience)
- [ ] trained small group leader

Study Guide and Group Process

Please check items that describe the material in the study guide:
- [ ] varied
- [ ] monotonous
- [ ] creative
- [ ] dull
- [ ] clear
- [ ] unclear
- [ ] interesting to participants
- [ ] uninteresting to participants
- [ ] too much
- [ ] too little
- [ ] helpful, stimulating
- [ ] not helpful or stimulating
- [ ] overly complex, long
- [ ] appropriate level of difficulty

Please check items that describe the group sessions:
- [ ] lively
- [ ] dull
- [ ] dominated by leader
- [ ] involved most participants
- [ ] relevant to lives of participants
- [ ] irrelevant to lives of participants
- [ ] worthwhile
- [ ] not worthwhile

In general I would rate this material as

☐ excellent
☐ very good
☐ good
☐ fair
☐ poor

Additional comments on any aspect of this Bible study:

Name (optional): _____
Church: _____
_____
City/State/Province: _____
_____

Please send completed form to

Word Alive / Luke (Part One)
Faith Alive Christian Resources
2850 Kalamazoo Ave. SE
Grand Rapids, MI 49560

Thank you!